Affordable Exhibition Design

Affordable Exhibition Design

Francesc Zamora Mola

COLLINS DESIGN

An Imprint of HarperCollins *Publishers*

AFFORDABLE EXHIBITION DESIGN
Copyright © 2010 COLLINS DESIGN and LOFT Publications

HarperCollins books may be purchased for educational, business, or sales promotional use.
For information, please write: Special Markets Department, HarperCollins*Publishers*,
10 East 53rd Street, New York, NY 10022.

First Edition published in 2010 by
Collins Design
An Imprint of HarperCollins*Publishers*
10 East 53rd Street
New York, NY 10022
Tel.: (212) 207-7000
Fax: (212) 207-7654
collinsdesign@harpercollins.com
www.harpercollins.com

Distributed throughout the world by
HarperCollins*Publishers*
10 East 53rd Street
New York, NY 10022
Fax: (212) 207-7654

Packaged by
LOFT Publications
Via Laietana 32, 4o Of. 92
08003 Barcelona, Spain
Tel.: +34 932 688 088
Fax: +34 932 687 073
loft@loftpublications.com
www.loftpublications.com

Editorial coordination:
Simone K. Schleifer

Assistant editorial coordination:
Aitana Lleonart Triquell

Editor:
Francesc Zamora Mola

Art director:
Mireia Casanovas Soley

Design and layout coordination:
Claudia Martínez Alonso

Layout:
Cristina Simó Perales

Cover design:
María Eugenia Castell Carballo

Library of Congress Control Number: 2010935072
ISBN: 978-0-06-196882-2

Printed in Spain

Contents

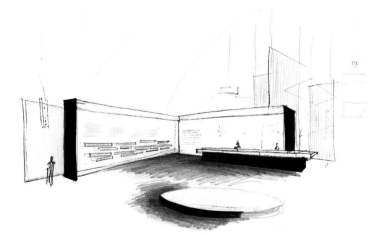

A good design is crucial for the success of an exhibition stand, which is ultimately made to impress. Needless to say, there are many other decisive elements that contribute to this success, but form, layout, and visuals are all very important. Particularly for trade events, where stands need to make a strong impression, exhibitors know that a striking stand is as important as the product displayed.

Professionals who specialize in the design of exhibition stands take into account factors that drive their decisions throughout the design process. For instance, the choice of materials depends on answering questions such as: How fast can the stand be assembled? How easy should it be to manipulate? And how much material is disposed of at the end of the event? While it is true that renting a modular stand is a convenient and in most cases more affordable option for a temporary need, a custom-designed stand offers the possibility of a unique solution limited only by imagination and budget.

A custom design may not be as affordable as a generic modular stand, such as those available from global suppliers of exhibition and display equipment, but it is the ultimate solution to convey brand and marketing philosophies and strategies. More and more exhibitors who attend different fairs during the course of a year

or repeatedly attend the same fair every year choose the option of investing in an exhibition stand that can be reused. Exhibitors rely on the effectiveness of their stands to attract new prospects and customers and to help them stand out from their competitors. The way the graphic information is presented is essential in the process of attracting and holding the visitors' attention, and eventually delivering the desired messages.

And so exhibitors turn to designers who know the technical processes to fabricate a functional stand, have a sensible understanding of media art, and possess a great amount of creative talent.

A stand is considered successful when it has fulfilled its function at the time of the exhibition and is remembered when the show has ended. The conceptual idea and the quality of the construction contribute to the fulfillment of this objective, along with materials, lighting, colors, graphics, and the presentation of the products or services. While the budget limits the range of possible materials and construction solutions, designers take it as a challenge in producing highly visual designs. The stands included in the book demonstrate that the best stand designs are not necessarily expensive. "Projektpilot" by D'ART DESIGN GRUPPE and "Cardboard Cloud" by Fantastic Norway are proof

that astonishing results can be achieved with common materials such as cardboard tubes and boxes.

Also, a number of the stand designs presented in this book include considerations of sustainability. While developing the design concept, the aesthetic appearance, and the functional aspects of the stand, designers integrate sustainable principles early in the design process to determine the environmental impact of the stand during its construction, use, and disposal. This ensures that the design satisfies the requirements without too much excess of materials. A successful stand considers the 3 R's from its conception: reduce, reuse, and recycle.

Lighting consumes a lot of energy, but it is essential in exhibition halls. While stands need to be appropriately lit, selecting energy-efficient lights allows their designs to be more environmentally friendly. Similarly, reducing waste by using materials that can be reused or recycled, maximizing the use of prefabricated stand parts, and reducing the on-site construction of new materials not only saves money but also allows for quick installation and dismounting processes.

Many of the stands featured in the book have been designed with components that, in most cases, will be reused. The stand that

Haag Wagner designed for the Swiss Society of Engineers and Architects effectively captures the connection with the construction industry and responds to the client's requirement to have a stand for long-term use that also expresses a sustainability concept. Another clear example of a successful stand that has fulfilled its function at the time of the exhibition and found a new use outside the context of the trade fair event is "Jenga'em." A modular piece designed by Dylan Kwok and Yuko Takagi turned stand for the 2007 edition of the Finnish Biannual Furniture Fair, Jenga'em found its new home at the Goethe Institute Helsinki right after the exhibition.

Even before an event starts, there is a lot of activity in the exhibition hall, and this repeats again at the end, when dismounting begins. All of this is so that for a few days the stands will look their best for presentation to visitors.

The exhibition designs featured in this book have been specifically chosen for their innovative designs, effective visual communication, affordable construction costs, environmentally-friendly elements, and ability to impress clients. Their images and descriptions can be used as inspiration for your exhibition designs.

IPEVO Cardboard Booth

Taipei, Taiwan December 1–9, 2007

© Marc Gerritsen

Taiwan-USA based IPEVO is a young Internet hardware company that creates unique, award-winning products made for emergent Web behaviors. To extend the client's design-driven brand philosophy, XRANGE created a unique 775 sq ft corrugated cardboard booth that could be completely recycled after the nine-day exhibition. The design concept was a deliberate move to counter the prevalent use-and-toss excesses of expo mentality, and to create a unique brand experience for IPEVO with an intended environmental sensitivity without resorting to generic modular, space-framed booth constructions.

Recycled corrugated cardboard was used as structure, surface finish, and display settings in order to convey a high level of coherence and finesse to the booth despite the rough and pliable nature of the material. To further minimize waste, hollow structures were used for greater material efficiency and structural rigidity. "Base pallets" with a 1-ton load capacity formed the structural floor and stage while stacked lighter-weight "stand pallets" formed the main display islands for the products, with their slotted structure doubling as storage for flyers. Life-size cutout user scenario "stories" complemented the products as backdrops.

Show: **2007 Taipei IT Month Expo**
Category: **Trade show detail**
Designer: **XRANGE**
Client: **IPEVO**
Area: **775 sq ft**
Cost: **$10,000**

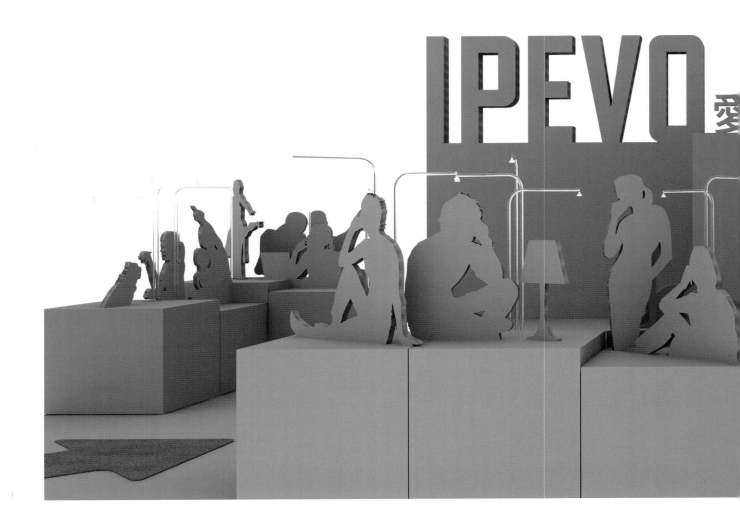

The display islands were lightweight hollow core pallets that allowed easy running of sizable cables and storage of printed material. The life-size silhouettes suggest scenarios: conferencing, meeting, presentation, leisure, away from the computer, etc.

Pickles & Chutney

Fort Mason Pavilion, San Francisco, CA, USA
August 29–31, 2008

© Matthew Millan

The 2008 edition of Slow Food Nation, the country's first major sustainable foods celebration, took place over Labor Day weekend at Fort Mason in San Francisco. Individual "Taste Pavilions" fabricated from repurposed materials were designed by the Bay Area's most prominent design firms. Sagan Piechota's design for the "Pickle-and-Chutney" booth—assembled just days before the event—featured walls made of pickle jars and an undulating ceiling composed of 3,024 mason jar lids suspended with filament, Velcro, and earring backs.

The "walls" were created by multiple rows of jars simply attached to wood studs and arranged to encourage visitor participation by taking and leaving recipes showcased within the jars.

Over the course of a month and ten laborious building sessions, more than one hundred volunteers contributed their time, effort, ideas, and stories to the completion of the booth. The team spirit generated throughout this journey would become the most valuable aspect of the participants' involvement and distinctly reflective of the Slow Food movement.

Show: **Slow Food Nation 2008**
Category: **Trade show design**
Designer: **Sagan Piechota**
Client: **Slow Food Nation**
Area: **792 sq ft**
Cost: **$6,000**

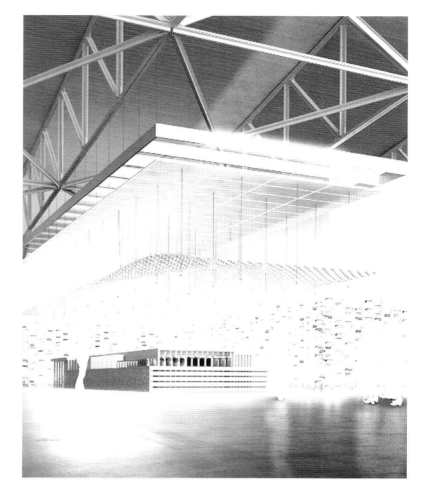

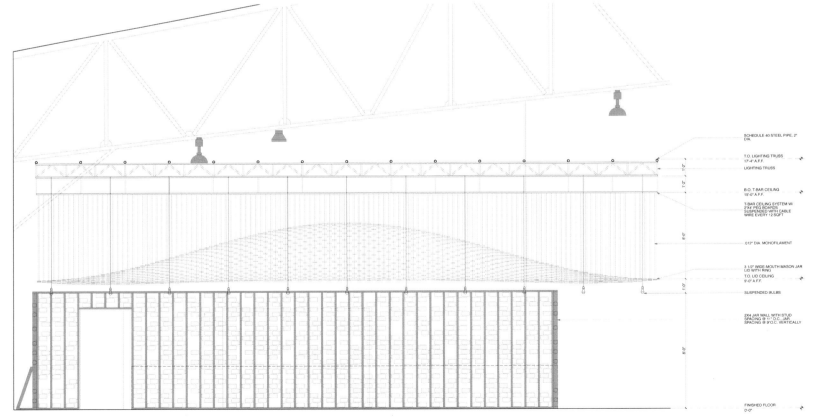

Long elevation

SCHEDULE 40 STEEL PIPE, 2" DIA.

T.O. LIGHTING TRUSS
17'-4" A.F.F.

LIGHTING TRUSS

B.O. T-BAR CEILING
15'-0" A.F.F.

T-BAR CEILING SYSTEM W/ 2X4 PEG BOARDS SUSPENDED WITH CABLE WIRE EVERY 12 SQFT

.012" DIA. MONOFILAMENT

3 1/2" WIDE-MOUTH MASON JAR LID WITH RING

T.O. LID CEILING
9'-0" A.F.F.

SUSPENDED BULBS

2X4 JAR WALL WITH STUD SPACING @ 1" O.C., JAR SPACING @ 9'O.C. VERTICALLY

FINISHED FLCOR
0'-0"

Garden Vision

**Frankfurt am Main, Germany
February 12–16, 2010**

© D'ART DESIGN GRUPPE

At the 2010 edition of Ambiente, an international consumer-goods event, everything revolved around tableware, kitchenware and household goods, gift items and decorations, as well as home and furnishing accessories.

At a time when gardens have ceased to be an appendage to the house and have become a living-area extension of the home, the firms Weber, Kettler, Lechuza, and Scheurich decided on a joint venture with the signature name of "Garden Vision." The idea behind the colorful setting was to unite BBQ culture and recreational activities with high living standards. D'ART DESIGN GRUPPE has brought the design of the stand to life in the form of an imaginative garden landscape as if seen through a magnifying glass. The stand was installed in the center of the hall, and its success with visitors derived from a comical vision of a blooming meadow with larger-than-life bright green grass shoots (some over 13 feet tall), long plant stalks, colorful butterflies, and a fly agaric mushroom as the centerpiece. The names of the four collaborating firms were printed on circles of different colors that represented flowers.

The designers were able to create a cost-effective stand design without losing any attention to detail.

Show: **Ambiente 2010**
Category: **Trade show design**
Designer: **D'ART DESIGN GRUPPE**
Client: **Garden Vision (Weber, Kettler, Lechuza, Scheurich)**
Area: **517 sq ft**
Cost: **Not available**

In the center of the stand, under the fly agaric mushroom, firm representatives presented their innovative products and served refreshments while TV monitors placed throughout the stand played information for more informal presentations.

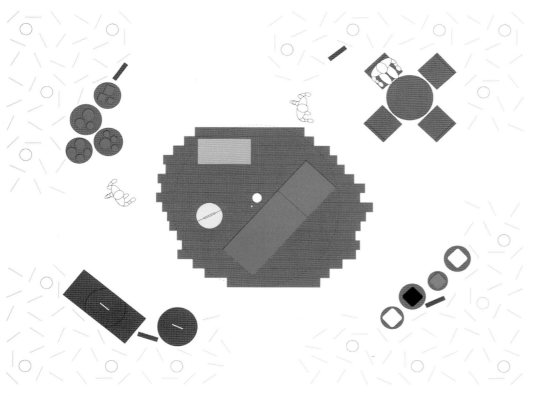

Stand plan

POL Oxygen

Melbourne, Australia April 19–21, 2007

© Kevin Hui

The design for *POL Oxygen* magazine took the award for "Best stand design" at Australia's biggest design fair, designEX, held in Melbourne. DesignEx is the leading event for the interior design and architecture industry.

For the 2007 edition of this event, *POL Oxygen* teamed up with Andrew Maynard and Brad Holt from Andrew Maynard Architects—one of Melbourne's most talked about and creative architectural firms. The design consisted of a narrow 39.4 x 6.5 ft space transformed into a lush green nature strip; a retreat away from the trade fair environment.

Unfortunately, shortly after, POL Publications discontinued all its publications, among which was *POL Oxygen*, an award-winning international design, art, and architecture quarterly magazine. *POL Oxygen* won numerous awards for art, design, and production, including Best Art and Design magazine and Best Art Direction in show at the FOLIO Show in New York.

Show: **designEX**
Category: **Trade show design**
Designer: **Andrew Maynard Architects**
Client: ***POL Oxygen* magazine**
Area: **258 sq ft**
Cost: **AUS$80,000 (includes donated materials)**

The stand therefore was a conceptual representation of nature, inspiration, "oxygen," and in the context of the fair, also the material for the three pillars of *POL Oxygen* magazine: design, art, and architecture.

Design Post Cologne by Quinze & Milan

Cologne, Germany 2006-2008

© Quinze & Milan

Reminiscent of the "Uchronia" colossal matchstick sculpture at the Burning Man Festival in the Nevada desert in 2006, Arne Quinze developed a wooden structure on one of the mezzanine levels of the Design Post building in Cologne. The installation for Design Post offered an exciting exhibition space that encompassed different zones used by internationally renowned design companies. With this dynamic creation came the presentation of the firm's own new product: CLUB, a simple, bold, and colorful line of seating for both indoor and outdoor use made from Quinze & Milan's proprietary QM FOAM™. Of the wood-studded sculpture, Quinze explained, "It resembles a frozen movement, speed caught in time. It is a powerful means of communication—if you look at it from a distance, pure movement seems to keep the volatile structure in the air." As for the used wood, the creator assured that every piece of wood was fully reused and recycled.

As part of an ongoing design experience, Quinze also designed "Cityscape," a similar structure to be built this year in Brussels; a 39.4-ft-tall similar sculpture. People will be able to walk under it and experience the light and shadow effects cast on the pavement.

Show: **Permanent Quinze & Milan showroom at Design Post Cologne**
Category: **Trade show design**
Designer: **Quinze & Milan**
Client: **Design Post**
Area: **250 m²**
Cost: **Not available**

The installation interacted with the original steel structure of the historically significant 1913 post office building. In total, the construction required six miles of wood, fifty thousand nails, and eighteen boxes of polyester.

Identity De/Coding

Copenhagen, Denmark 2005

© Anders Sune Berg

What does identity mean for the design of a chair? "Identity De/Coding" was a project that focused on what design stands for: identity. The installation began at the entrance of the Copenhagen International Furniture Fair. There, visitors were encouraged to choose one of five identities that correspond to the different visitors' profiles and adopt it for the duration of the visit. The different profiles were depicted on banners in the vestibule. Every visitor was then assigned a key strap in one of five colors— yellow, light blue, brown, orange or pink—before starting to follow the corresponding colored path. The key strap served as identification and at the same time functioned as a personal souvenir from "Identity De/Coding". In the center of the hall was "Grasslandscape," a furniture-free area with a café, a stage, a sound theater, and INDEX: stand. INDEX: was all about ideas; about how design can improve our lives. What if one did not like being categorized as a given type? A visit to the INDEX: stand for "decoding" freed visitors from any categorizing tie. In sum, Copenhagen International Furniture Fair was in that occasion an interactive experience.

Show: **Copenhagen International Furniture Fair**
Category: **Trade show design**
Designer: **Bosch & Fjord**
Client: **Bella Center and Copenhagen International Furniture Fair**
Area: **Not available**
Cost: **Not available**

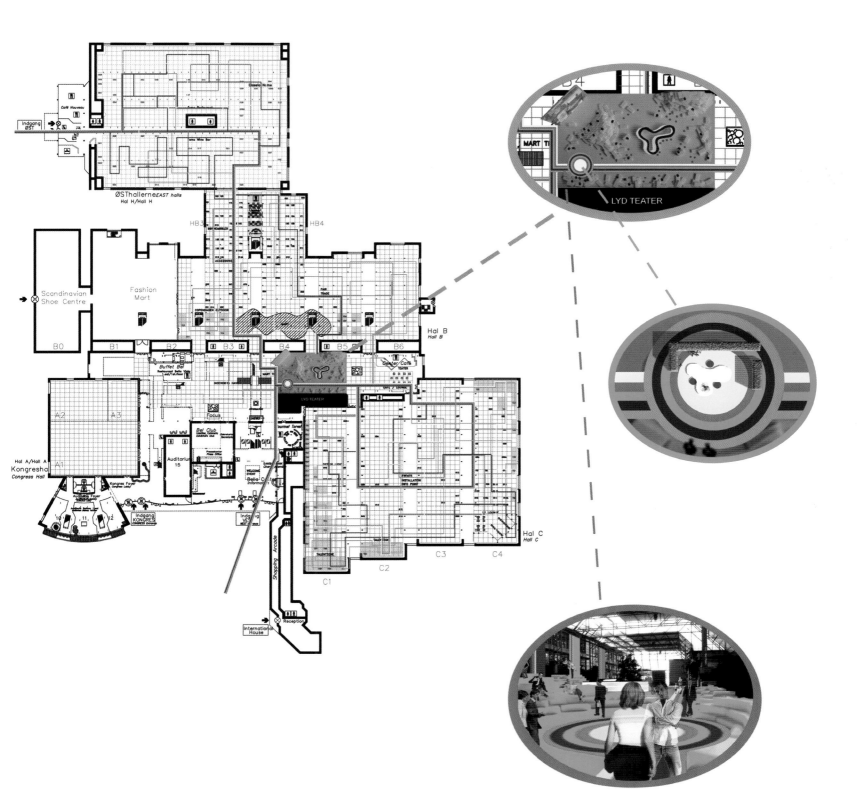

Exhibition hall plan

Coop Stand

Milan, Italy May 8–10 2007

© Saverio Lombardi Vallauri, Milano

Since 2004, Coop, the leading Italian supermarket chain, has offered all of its suppliers the opportunity to take some concrete actions in specific domains such as environmental protection, the defence of human rights, and nutritional safety. This stand was motivated by the ECR-Italy project dealing with Corporate Social Responsibility. In anticipation of its yearly participation in the forum, Coop trusted the design of its stand to the Milan-based vc a, who had already designed the new in-store image and communication of the company's supermarket.

The institutional colors—white and red—were matched in a rational mix of volumes and surfaces. Against this composition, two recurrent metaphors were staged, namely *bond* and *embrace*, which immediately reminded the visitor of the company's value-focused approach. Reproduced on the floor as a blown-up decorative pattern, the logo was the hallmark of the four exhibit areas, respectively dedicated to "fair" products, research in product design, handling of fresh products, and Coop-branded products. The large bottom wall evoked and magnified the theme of bonding values and relations. A crowded reception and sampling area, livened up by the presence of people, completed the space layout.

Show: **ECR Europe Forum & Marketplace**
Category: **Trade show design**
Designer: **vc a / Paolo Cesaretti + Cristiana Vannini**
Client: **Coop Italia**
Area: **Approx. 3,229 sq ft**
Cost: **Not available**

PROPOSTA A

COOP / ECR. MILANO.

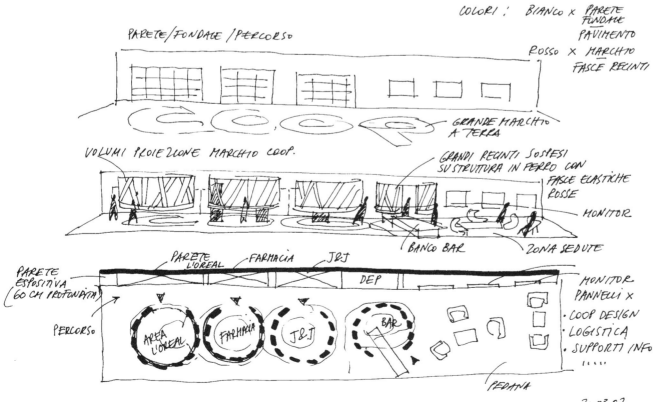

COLORI: BIANCO x PARETE FONDALE PAVIMENTO

ROSSO x MARCHIO FASCE RECINTI

PARETE/FONDALE/PERCORSO

C O O P — GRANDE MARCHIO A TERRA

VOLUMI PROIEZIONE MARCHIO COOP.

GRANDI RECINTI SOSPESI SU STRUTTURA IN FERRO CON FASCE ELASTICHE ROSSE

MONITOR

BANCO BAR — ZONA SEDUTE

PARETE ESPOSITIVA (60 CM PROFONDITÀ)

PERCORSO

PARETE L'OREAL — FARMACIA — J&J

DEP

MONITOR PANNELLI x
• COOP DESIGN
• LOGISTICA
• SUPPORTI INFO
.....

AREA L'OREAL — FARMACIA — J&J — BAR

PEDANA

20.03.07

LINEA SOLIDAL coop.

Scegliere i prodotti a marchio Coop della linea solidal è una buona azione per chi compra e per il sud del mondo. Ogni prodotto infatti, viene acquistato in alcuni paesi dell'Asia, Africa, Centro e Sud America da produttori che garantiscono ai lavoratori salari e condizioni di vita adeguati, non utilizzano lavoro minorile, rispettano i diritti sindacali e non operano alcuna discriminazione. In più, parte dei guadagni è reinvestita in progetti per lo sviluppo delle comunità locali.

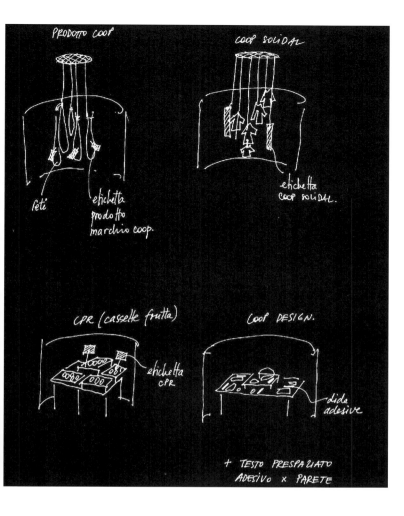

The institutional vocation was the theme to be communicated alongside values such as membership, solidarity, and sustainability, which have always distinguished the work of Coop and stand for its number-one communication tool.

Count-it

Amsterdam, Netherlands 2002

© Eugeni Pons

In spite of the tight budget and the reduced area available to build the stand, Maurice Mentjens Design found a strategy so that the presence of Inabase at Highlife would be as eye-catching as possible. The "Count-it" cash desk system was specially developed for the iMac, and so it made perfect sense that the stand would be all white. A sophisticated lighting system was used to project different colors onto the white surfaces and continuously change the atmosphere of the stand.

The stand, composed of prefabricated elements that could be reused and that allowed for the reconfiguration of the layout, was mounted and dismounted with ease. The simplicity of the plan and the use of few elements expressed an image of order.

Rather than following an open configuration, commonly used in the design of stands, "Count-it" presented a cage-like appearance by means of thick plastic rods that delimited the stand and separated the different areas, which included a reception area, a meeting room, and an area with a kitchen unit. Suspended from a steel structure, the tubes lightly brushed the floor and conveyed an impression of strength and security.

Show: **Highlife**
Category: **Trade show design**
Designer: **Maurice Mentjens Design**
Client: **Inabase**
Area: **301.4 sq ft**
Cost: **Not available**

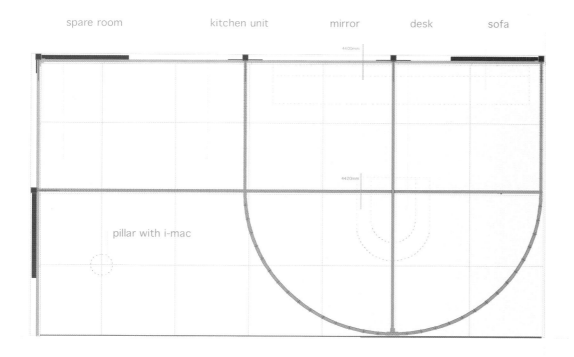

spare room   kitchen unit   mirror   desk   sofa

4400mm

4420mm

pillar with i-mac

Stand plan

Strong magnets mounted to the bottom of each tube and underneath the flooring attracted each other. Whenever a visitor entered or exited the stand and pushed a tube to one side, the tube quickly swung back to its original position.

Vitra stand

Milan, Italy April 13–18, 2005

© Miro Zagnoli , R & E Bouroullec

Designed by Ronan & Erwan Bouroullec, "Algues" is a modular component to form creative space dividers of any shape and size. These plastic modules constituted the conceptual basis of the stand for Vitra at Pelota, a former sports arena in Milan's Brera area. A series of space dividers similar to oversized office cubicles were mounted along the circulation paths. But behind this simple geometric plan, the design was a carefully considered study of scale, color, and texture. In fact what one could perceive at first sight as a continuous, seamless suspended surface was actually a composition of many plastic components assembled together — similar in shape but not in color. The designs of these plastic curtains presented variations in color combinations and patterns and also in texture; the different zone dividers created a regular undulating texture because the basic modular element was angular. In contrast, a free-form white sheet made of an organically shaped module was draped over various zones. The designers were successful in creating a visually outstanding backdrop for Vitra composed uniquely of the design company's product, which at the end of the show was packed up and reused.

Show: **La Pelota Sports Center**
Category: **Trade show design**
Designer: **Ronan & Erwan Bouroullec**
Client: **Vitra**
Area: **Not available**
Cost: **Not available**

The success of this installation derived from the fact that the product itself was also the display. A clever solution that fulfilled the necessity for a unique stand material and also served as a marketing strategy to present one of Vitra's products.

AMI Booth

Düsseldorf, Germany October 2004

© Caramel Architekten

This simple stand presented two ways of access, while the red carpet reinforced the idea of entry. The colors of the textile surfaces and the triple loop echoed the company's logo.

Visually striking in both its shape and its colors, the stand offered various degrees of exposure to the immediate surroundings. But in fact, the initial idea was to create a secluded space for meetings, isolated from the activity around it. The spatial structure was one single freestanding object framed by standard white screens that carried only the letters of the company logo. The stand's functions took place within this freestanding object and around it: in the interior, there was a row of presentation tables where visitors could meet with the company's representatives.

Opposite these tables, hanging screens played AMI's information. Viewers could sit comfortably on fold-out chairs that "peeled off" from the face of the loop.

Lighting was a key element of this stand's design and contributed to the relaxed environment: Two rails crossing the triple loop lengthwise reinforced the access ways and served as supports for technical requirements that included a mandatory sprinkler system and indirect lighting.

Show: **K04**
Category: **Trade show design**
Designer: **Caramel Architekten with Fritz Stiper**
Client: **Agrolinz Melamine International**
Area: **1,076.40 sq ft**
Cost: **€100,000**

| storage | consulting | presentation tables | interactive information | recreation/
extra consulting | textil wall |

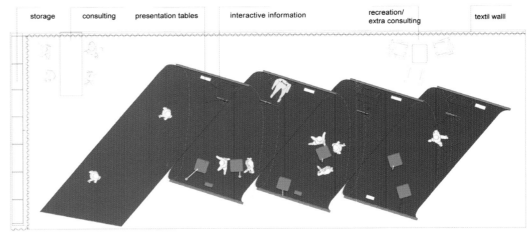

floor

Stand plan and elevation

The triple-loop structure was formed by a lightweight wooden construction consisting of five prefabricated parts per loop. The structure, covered with a layer of felt-like material and an imitation black leather finish, was built to be easily assembled and reused.

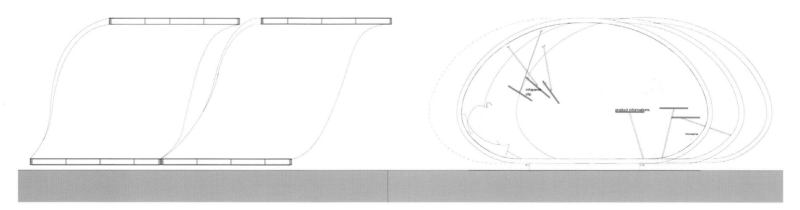

Sections

uboot.com

Düsseldorf, Germany September 2007

© Hackenbroich Architekten

The company uboot.com provides an Internet platform for a youth network with blogs, galleries, and videos. For the Online Marketing trade show, the company desired a stand with a lounge atmosphere adequate for the business environment, but with an innovative configuration representing the youth groups of Internet social networks.

The design was based on a single volume hovering above the stand. This volume consisted of 1,280 white ribbons of different lengths suspended from the ceiling. The ends of the ribbons formed a surface that created differentiated areas with varying levels of privacy. The ribbons formed a giant lampshade to reflect the light. The composition acted more as a filter than a barrier and endowed the ceiling with a permeable character.

Besides the lounge atmosphere of this trade fair stand, the design presented an analogy to Internet. The undulating "ceiling" composed of individual elements contributed to the creation of different atmospheres just like the Web 2.0 which generates the different digital networks by means of individual contributions.

Show: **Online Marketing**
Category: **Trade show design**
Designer: **Hackenbroich Architekten**
Client: **uboot.com mobile Internet services**
Area: **560 sq ft**
Cost: **€18,000**

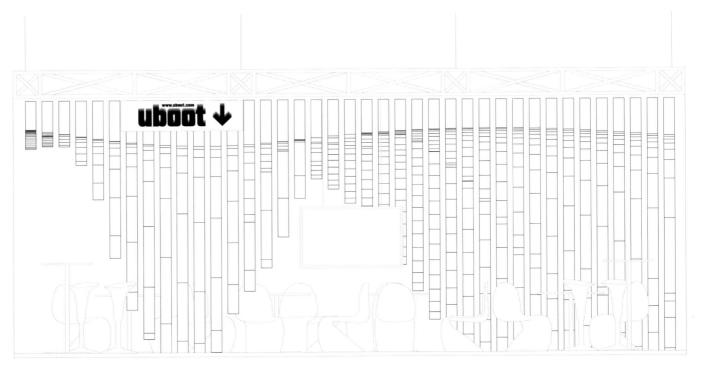

Elevation

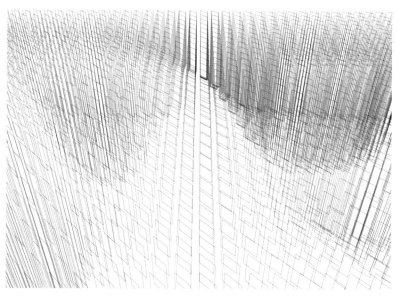

Modulated surface

The atmosphere of the stand was dominated by the softness and the movement of the textile ribbons, which were almost as intangible as the Internet itself. After the fair, they were taken down and recycled, leaving behind only filaments.

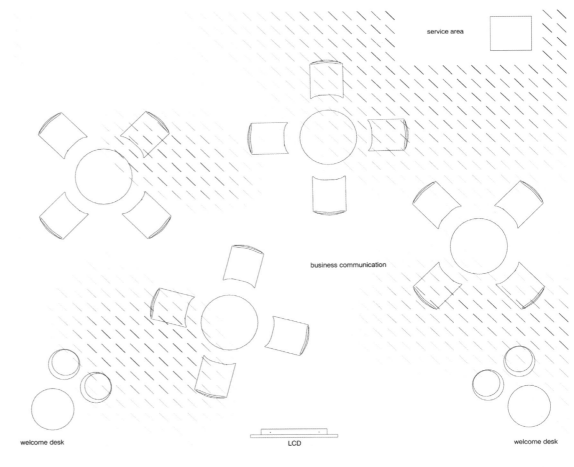

service area

business communication

welcome desk

LCD

welcome desk

Stand plan

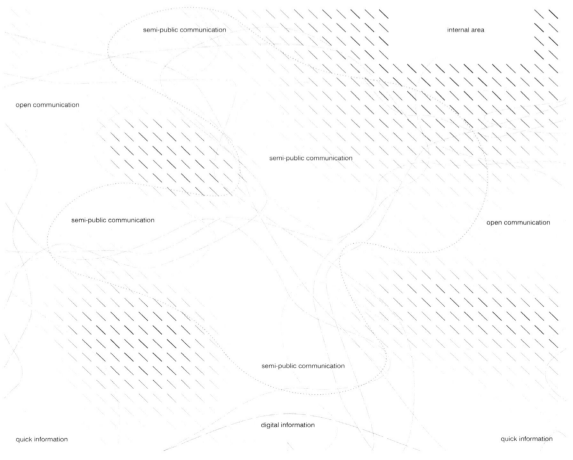

semi-public communication

internal area

open communication

semi-public communication

semi-public communication

open communication

semi-public communication

digital information

quick information

quick information

Zone diagram

Garment Garden

Messe Frankfurt, Germany May 6–10, 2006

© Constantin Meyer Photographie and J. MAYER H. Architects

Nya Nordiska is dedicated to the design of innovative textiles, some of which have been the recipient of prestigious awards. The beginnings of the company were strongly influenced by the Scandinavian School of Design, and the stand that J. Mayer H. Architects developed for the occasion of the first Design Annual in Frankfurt reflected these origins with geometric sculptures. Through the years, the collection had also been adopting design influences from different cultures. In the words of the designer, "Each city fabric needs space for nature and retreat." Garment Garden for Nya Nordiska offered a place for relaxation within the fair premises. Vertical columns, whose forms could be found somewhere between skyscrapers and trees, were covered with folded fabric. One reading could be that of a curtain wall of a high-rise building; another, the bark of a tree. Mirrored walls transformed the small stand into an infinite forest where visitors could stroll among the rich textures of Nya Nordiska's textiles.

Show: **The Design Annual – Inside: Urban**
Category: **Trade show design**
Designer: **J. MAYER H. Architects**
Client: **Nya Nordiska**
Area: **425.2 sq ft**
Cost: **Approx. €25,000**

Fabric sculpture structure

Caged Beauty

Kortrijk, Belgium October 13–22, 2006

© Moroso

For the Moroso showroom at the International Interior Biennial in Kortrijk, Belgium, Arne Quinze created a spectacular stand built of fiberglass and white polyester string rectangular cages of different sizes and proportions. Some of the cages contained fluorescent tubes. The stand actually seemed to be a three-dimensional "Tetris" game where blocks had fallen from above and stacked to create solids and voids through which passersby could take a glance at the products on display. The cages delimited the stand area, leaving the center clear for circulation, reunion, and for the display of products. They also formed shelves. Within the area of the stand, it was raining chairs: Arne Quinze used Ross Lovegrove's Supernatural line of chairs to introduce the technology of injection molding in glass fiber–reinforced polypropylene. Various designs in different colors added another layer of dynamism to the already animated black and white stand. The design of the stand was representative of the Supernatural chair, which was presented as a product that offered excellent value for money while perfectly in line with the collection of the firm.

Show: **Interieur Biennale**
Category: **Trade show design**
Designer: **Quinze & Milan**
Client: **Moroso**
Area: **Not available**
Cost: **Not available**

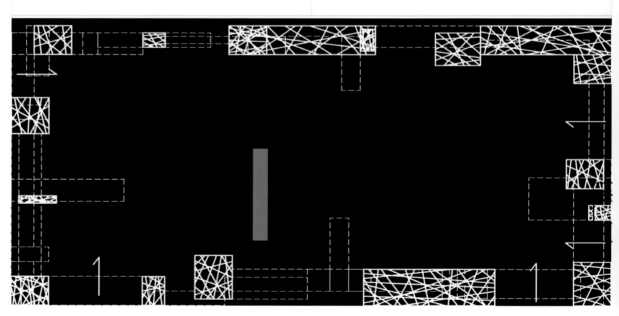

Stand plan

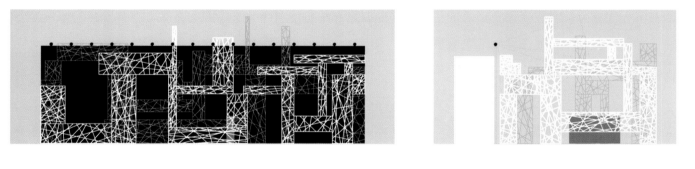

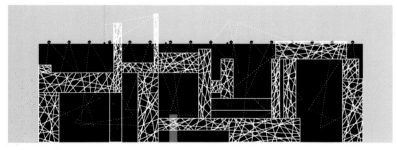
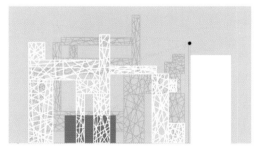

Stand elevations

SIA Schweizerischer Ingenieur- und Architektenverein (Swiss Society of Engineers and Architects)

Basel, Switzerland January 12–16, 2010

© Dominic Haag, HAAG WAGNER

The Swiss Society of Engineers and Architects surprised the visitors of the Swissbau 2010 with an unusual stand. As a result, the design was awarded the second prize in the best stand over 861 sq ft category. As a reference to the construction of concrete bearing walls, the stand was delimited by a series of trellises formed by offset layers of reinforcing mesh that provided for an exceptional visual presence at the building fair.

The booth was organized in four different areas of services: codes and regulations, continuing training, service, and law. Each area was defined by a color: red, blue, green, or yellow. This aesthetic solution functioned on two levels: In the context of the stand, the colors fulfilled a thematic organization of the products and services, reflecting the firm's culture; in the context of the fair, they served to attract the attention of the visitors.

Further, the client required a long-term use of the stand that would meet a sustainability objective. Lighting, an indispensable element, was used in the most efficient way possible. The steel frame and spruce wood elements required little treatment and 95 percent of this raw material was intended to be reused for other purposes after the fair.

Show: **Swissbau 2010**
Category: **Trade show design**
Designer: **Dominic Haag, HAAG WAGNER**
Client: **Schweizerischen Ingenieur- und Architektenverein SIA,**
Area: **861 sq ft**
Cost: **CHF 68,500**

The steel trellises created a visual effect that combined transparency and the massiveness of the material. To reinforce this effect, the trellises were lit in a theatrical way. The stand was erected on top of a technical floor that concealed all the wiring.

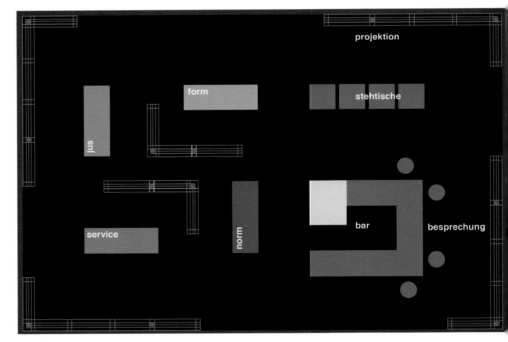

Stand plan

The designers were successful in showing how a compelling visual effect can be achieved while responding to a sustainable requirement and satisfying the client's requirement of a fair stand for long-term use.

Viabizzuno

Moscow, Russia 2005

© Viabizzuno

Viabizzuno is a design studio that often attracts attention for its spectacular lighting solutions. On the occasion of Interlight in Moscow, "Doccia Goccia" was the central piece in the layout of the stand: a sophisticated shower design in the shape of a water drop with incorporated lighting. This item was placed in the center of the booth, partly hidden by two modular partitions. Apparently, this seemed the only piece on display and the disposition of the elements that composed the stand added to the mysterious effect, since from outside the stand, one could hardly identify the water drop. Once in the stand, the visitor discovers the use of it and finds out that the modular partitions are also a Viabizzuno product: The small parts are shelf modules and cabinets that assembled together can become a functional space divider. The juxtaposition of the two products and the clever spatial organization reflected the versatility of this firm, which is able to offer a wide range of design solutions; from the most high-tech product to the simplest, most functional item.

Show: **Interlight**
Category: **Trade show design**
Designer: **Upo Architettura/Viabizzuno**
Client: **Viabizzuno**
Area: **Not available**
Cost: **Not available**

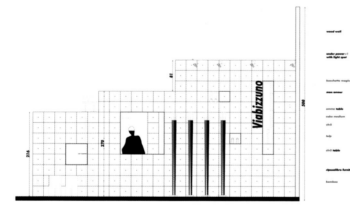

Front B

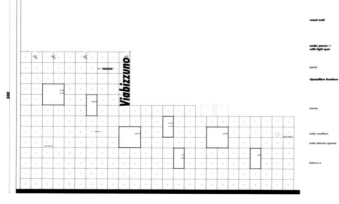

Front C

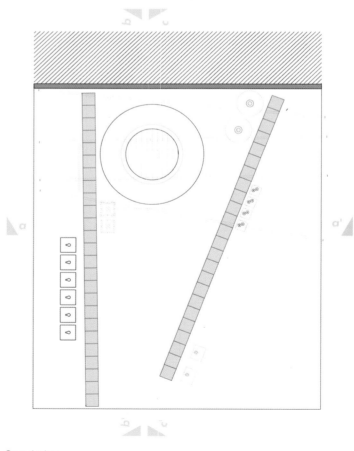

Stand plan

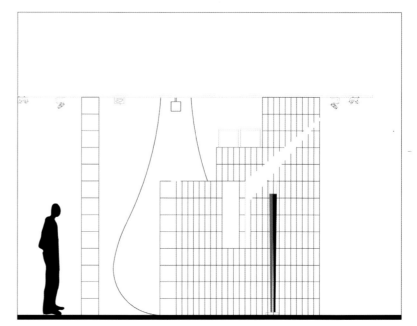

Section A

PASA / RAISIN   10µm IID30

INNOVACIÓN
F INNOVATION

PRESERVATION

HEATING

COOLING

DEHYDRATION AND DRYING

FERMENTATION

FERMENTACIÓN
FERMENTATION

CALOR HEAT

10.000
YEARS OF
INNOVATION

10.000
AÑOS DE
INNOVAC

© Eugeni Pons

Innoval '04

Barcelona, Spain 2005

Estudi Arola was commissioned to design the booth that would house Innoval 2004 at the Alimentaria Fair in Barcelona. The design had to include in the same space an exhibit of the Triptólemos Foundation featuring important events throughout the history of the food industry. The design presented the two programs separately: An antechamber presented the historic exhibition in a museum-like setting. This lead to an open area where Innoval products were displayed. This second part of the show was more representative of the "affordable" theme of this book.

The first section of the route was formed by rectangular boxes that combined showcases with objects and explanatory texts. The dominant color was black. Accent colors and an effective lighting system rounded off this museum context, which functioned as an antechamber to the more theatrical setting of the second part of the exhibit. The contained atmosphere of the museum section of the exhibition lead to an open space where the industrial shell of the building was exposed. The products were displayed on long banquet tables organized around a central mobile formed by translucent yellow plates.

Show: **Alimentaria**
Category: **Trade show design**
Designer: **Estudi Arola**
Client: **Innoval**
Area: **21,530 sq ft**
Cost: **Not available**

Exhibition plan

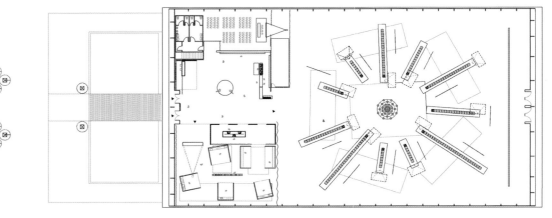

Visible from the entrance, this large suspended element acted as a visual lure. It was, however, difficult to discern what it was made of. Approaching this floating object entailed going through the historic exhibition.

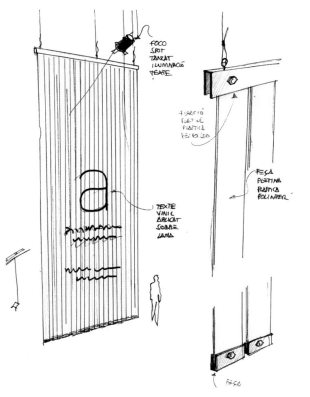

Design development sketches

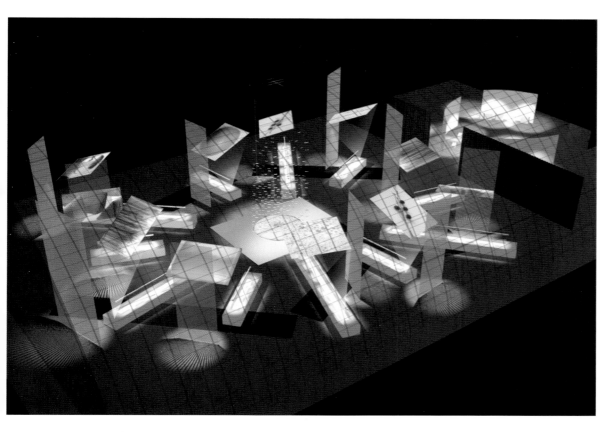

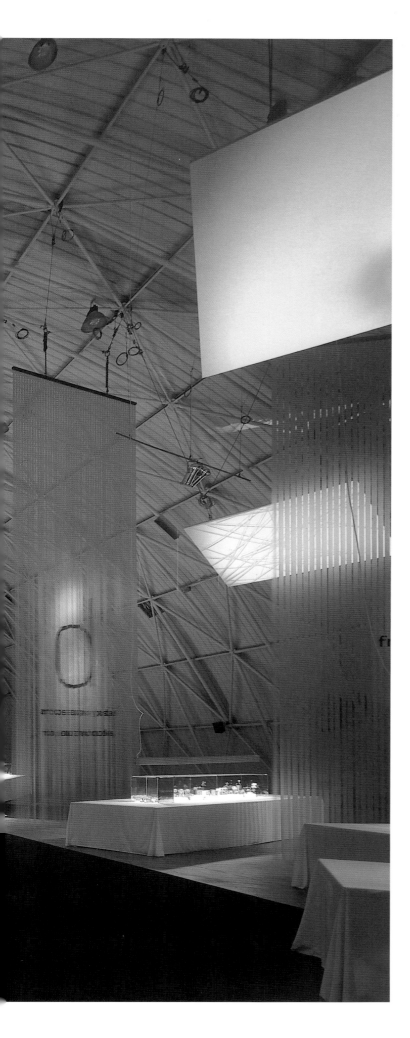

Lighting was a design element that added visual interest to the floating object, which first seemed like a giant ceiling lamp, then slowly, as one approached, became visible as plates suspended in the air as if the party guests had thrown them up.

Ibercon

Madrid, Spain 2004

© Eugeni Pons

BAAS's proposal for the Ibercon Booth at the Salón Inmobiliario de Madrid included the use of an unusual material to form a unique space that would stand out from the others. The aim was a budget-conscious design, easy to store and assemble, that at the same time would convey a sense of elegance and simplicity.

The booth was conceived as a continuous plane of ropes that formed the ceiling, the walls, and the supports for the various displays. This concept was realized by creating a steel structure onto which the ropes were stretched. The simple design was completed with a dark rug.

Three scale models were displayed as well as the construction documents of the company's most recent projects. Careful attention to detail was put into the presentation so that these elements would not interfere with the clean design of the booth. A selection of simple pieces of furniture was in line with the aesthetics of the booth: simple, light wood hemp chairs, classic Coderch ceiling lamps, and a large glass-top conference table filled the space and contributed to the desired effect.

Show: **Salón Inmobiliario de Madrid**
Category: **Trade show design**
Designer: **BAAS**
Client: **Ibercon**
Area: **861 sq ft**
Cost: **€57,600**

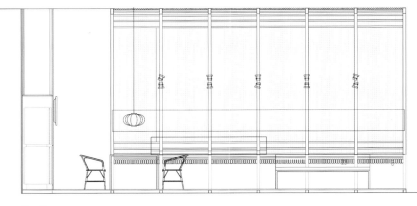

Section

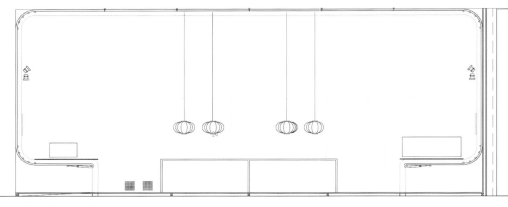

Frontal elevation

Adequate lighting set the atmosphere desired by the client, who was more interested in a comfortable space suitable for meetings than in a cumbersome showcase of products.

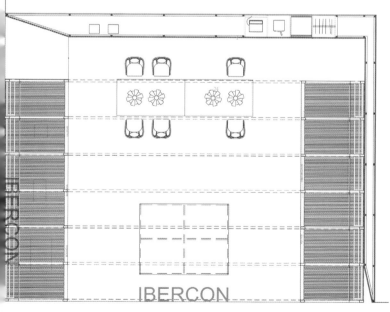

Stand plan

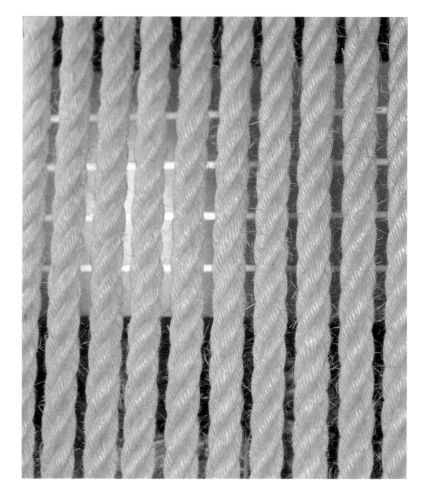

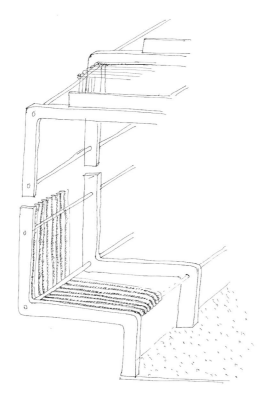

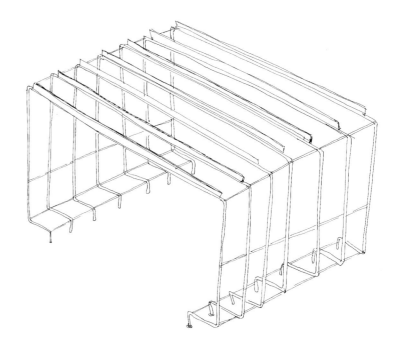

Sketches of the steel and rope stand structure

Jenga'em

Helsinki, Finland September 19–23, 2007

© Dylan Kwok

Jenga'em was an exhibit design dedicated to books and publications in general. It was based on a modular system that could be composed into numerous imaginative configurations. The versatility of this modular system allowed for storage, seating, and space dividing, and it encouraged activities such as reading and social interaction. The design, inspired by the wooden block game, resulted in a block-stacking spatial solution.

When assembled, the simple cubic elements (16 x 16 x 16 in) combine various functions: the double-sided bookshelf units optimize high-density shelving and at the same time can be used to organize spatial relationships; lighting is incorporated in one long block unit; benches of different sizes are available for seating and to support the stack of bookshelves. White birch, the Finnish national material, was chosen for both aesthetic and structural reasons. Birch plywood provided optimum strength for the construction, whereas birch viscose yarn excelled the unique beauty of the custom textile, which was woven for the seats and lampshade. Due to its hardwareless construction, Jenga'em could be transformed to adapt to any spatial requirements.

Show: **Finnish biannual furniture fair, Habitare**
Category: **Trade show design**
Designer: **Dylan Kwok and Yuko Takagi**
Client: **University of Art and Design**
Area: **118 x 94 ½ x 94 ½ in**
Cost: **€1,500 and donated materials**

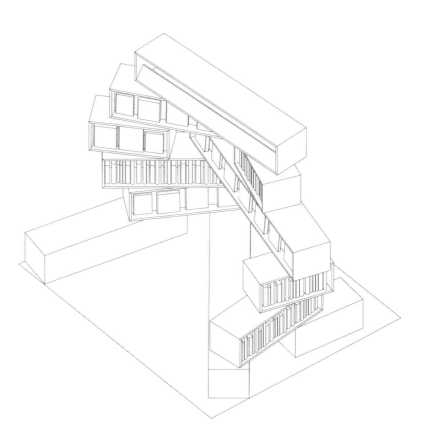

Axonometric

The idea was first launched at the Finnish biannual furniture fair, Habitare, in 2007. Unlike most exhibition design, the highly functional shelving system found a new home right after the exhibition, at the Goethe Institute Helsinki.

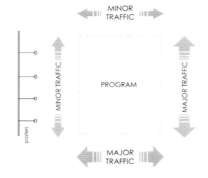

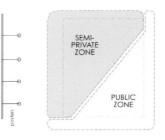

360° ACCESS
Freestanding proposal deserves 360° access from all directions.

TRAFFIC PATTERN
Traffic flow around the proposal varies according to its surroundings.

ZONES
Partitions help to define the spatial behavior.

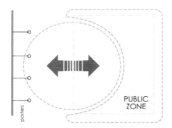

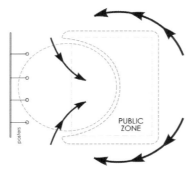

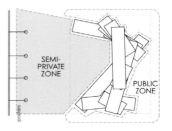

INTERACTION
A public area is generated by the interaction between the program and the posters.

ACTIVE FLOWS
The new semiprivate zone promotes active circulations and encourages visitors to sit in.

THE PROPOSAL
Jenga-ing the pieces according to the study

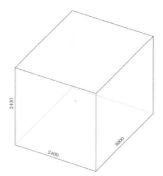

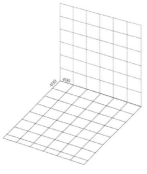

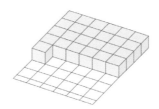

VOLUME
Size of the given area is 118 x 94 ½ x 94 ½ in

Dividing the plan with 16 x 16 in modules

10 meters of bookshelves = 25 units of 16 x 16 x 16 in

BOOKS BOOKS BOOKS
Fitting designed bookshelves into the program

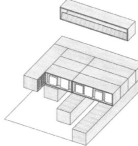

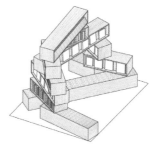

ELEVATION
Lifting bookshelves 15 ¾ in above ground for easy access

SUPPORTS
Introducing supporting elements Benches

ILLUMINATION
Crowning bookshelves with a light fixture on the top layer

JENGA'EM
Jenga-ing up the pieces to the maximum height

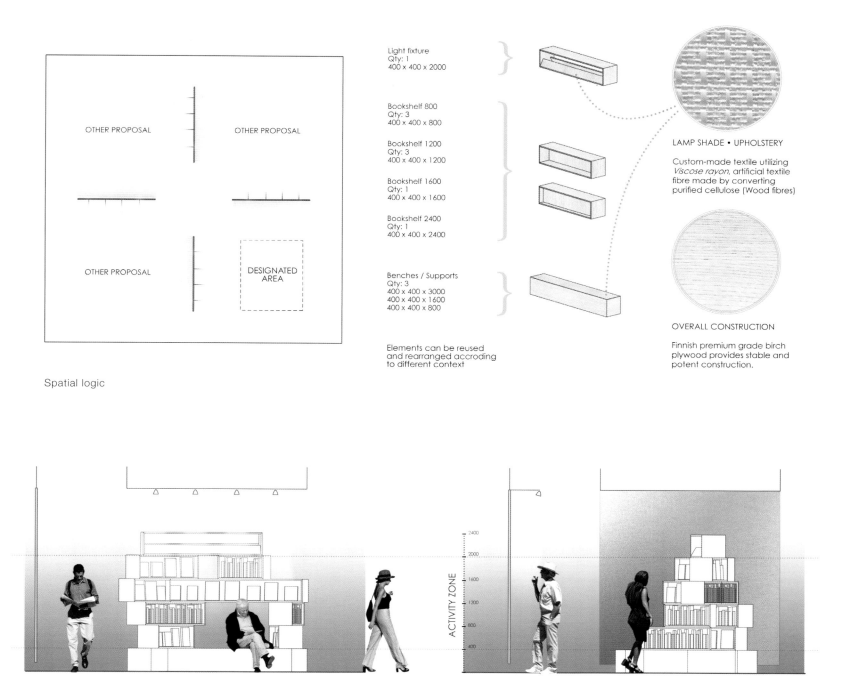

Light fixture
Qty: 1
400 x 400 x 2000

Bookshelf 800
Qty: 3
400 x 400 x 800

Bookshelf 1200
Qty: 3
400 x 400 x 1200

Bookshelf 1600
Qty: 1
400 x 400 x 1600

Bookshelf 2400
Qty: 1
400 x 400 x 2400

Benches / Supports
Qty: 3
400 x 400 x 3000
400 x 400 x 1600
400 x 400 x 800

Elements can be reused
and rearranged accroding
to different context

OTHER PROPOSAL

OTHER PROPOSAL

OTHER PROPOSAL

DESIGNATED
AREA

Spatial logic

LAMP SHADE • UPHOLSTERY

Custom-made textile utilizing
Viscose rayon, artificial textile
fibre made by converting
purified cellulose (Wood fibres)

OVERALL CONSTRUCTION

Finnish premium grade birch
plywood provides stable and
potent construction.

ACTIVITY ZONE

2400

2000

1600

1200

800

400

Elevations

Welkam

Düsseldorf, Germany February 23–27, 2008

© D'ART DESIGN GRUPPE

When one achieves unity out of contradictions, the result is eventually impressive. On the occasion of EuroShop 2008, D'ART DESIGN GRUPPE designed a stand for the German-Japanese firm Welkam and created a symbolic bridge between the two cultures. For its first time at EuroShop, Welkam required a stand that would make an impression at the fair and help position the firm in the international market. Welkam is a company that helps other firms introduce their products and services at fairs and events around the world. The architecture of the stand had its own identity: Inspired by Japanese characters, sheets of white folded paper formed a mobile that reinforced the cubic shape of the stand. As a counterpart to this playful element, a massive rectangular cabinet delimited the area of the stand. This combination caught the visitors' attention from a distance. While functional elements were integrated into the cabinets (drawers and boxes could be pulled out when needed), the center of the stand remained mostly free for circulation and communication, with the exception of a red table in the center as the heart of the stand.

Show: **EuroShop**
Category: **Trade show design**
Designer: **D'ART DESIGN GRUPPE**
Client: **Welkam**
Area: **387.5 sq ft**
Cost: **Not available**

Below the cloud of white sheets of paper, on top of the low red table, visitors could find information about the young company in the form of scrolls that were reminiscent of the traditional Japanese silk scrolls.

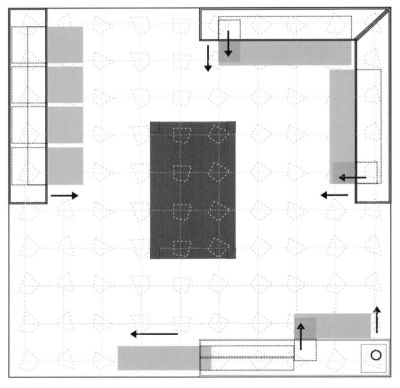

Stand plan

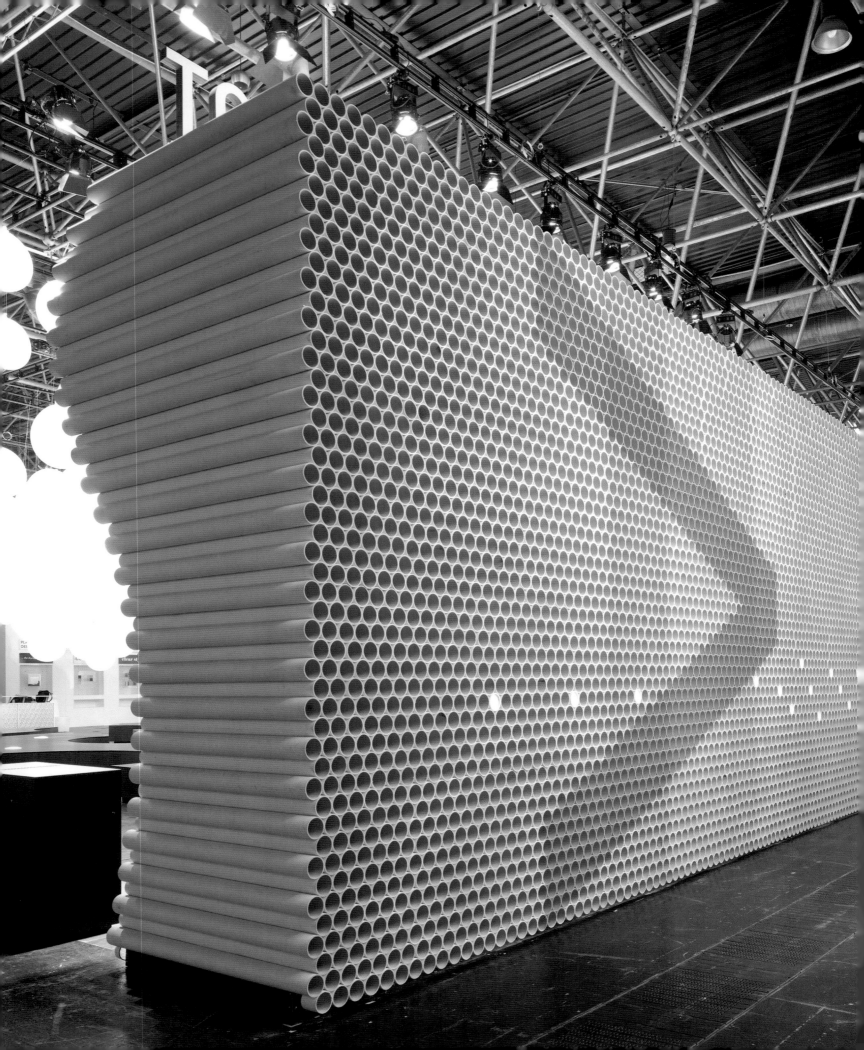

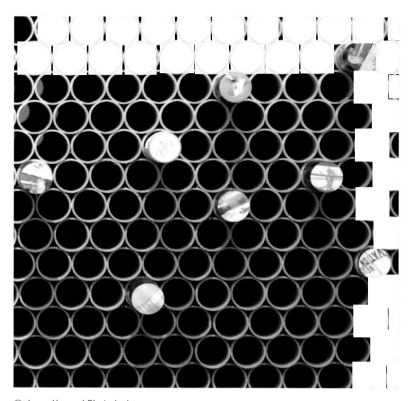

© Joerg Hempel Photodesign

Projektpilot

Düsseldorf, Germany
February 23–27, 2008

D'ART DESIGN GRUPPE created a spectacular exhibition stand at EuroShop for PROJEKTPILOT, a consulting firm that focuses on providing comprehensive services to advertising and design agencies. PROJEKTPILOT has been operating under its new name since January 2008 and was to present an extended range of services to an international public for the very first time at EuroShop.

Visitors to the company's unconventional exhibition stand could experience its philosophy and approach firsthand. The basic concept developed by D'ART DESIGN was to take a simple material such as cardboard out of its common context and use it for a different purpose. The result was an eye-catching stand that visitors would remember while associating PROJEKTPILOT with clever implementation.

There's extensive know-how behind this simple-looking construction, formed by a total of 8,140 cardboard tubes measuring over 6.2 miles in length, and weighing approximately 18 tons. Each tube had a specific length and a particular place in the 56-ft-long cardboard structure; no less than a meticulous and creative composition that reflects the philosophy of the company.

Show: **EuroShop**
Category: **Trade show design**
Designer: **D'ART DESIGN GRUPPE**
Client: **PROJEKTPILOT**
Area: **Approx. 538 sq ft**
Cost: **Not available**

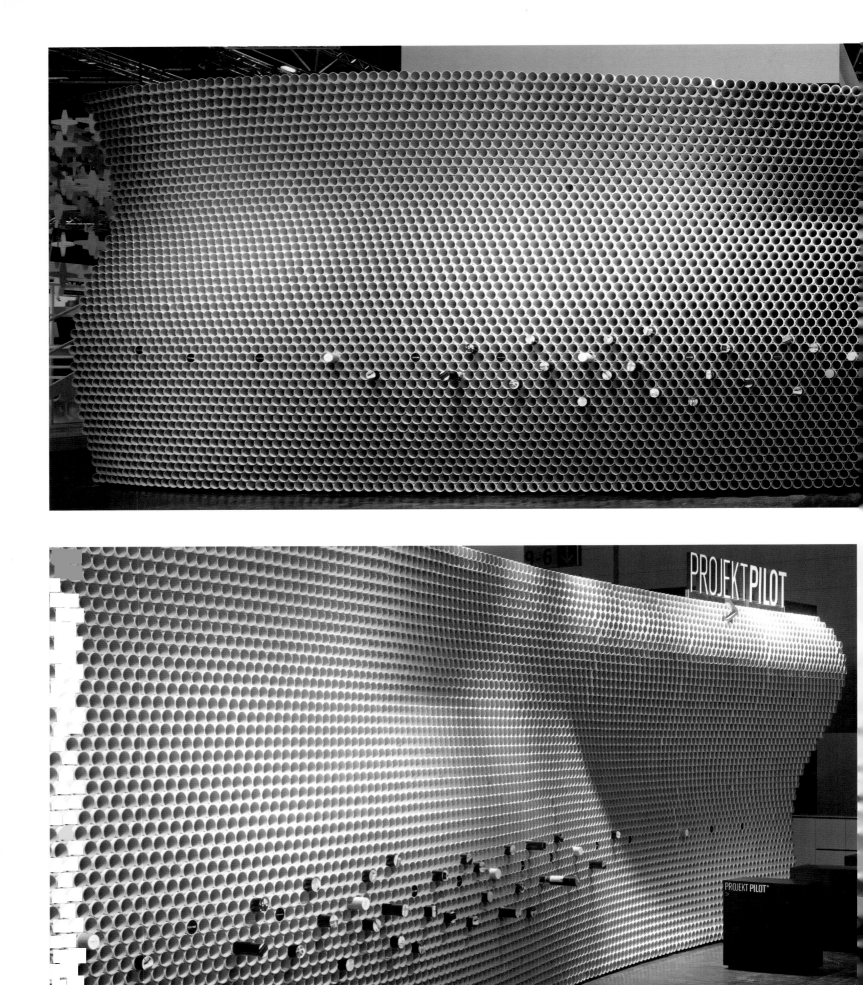

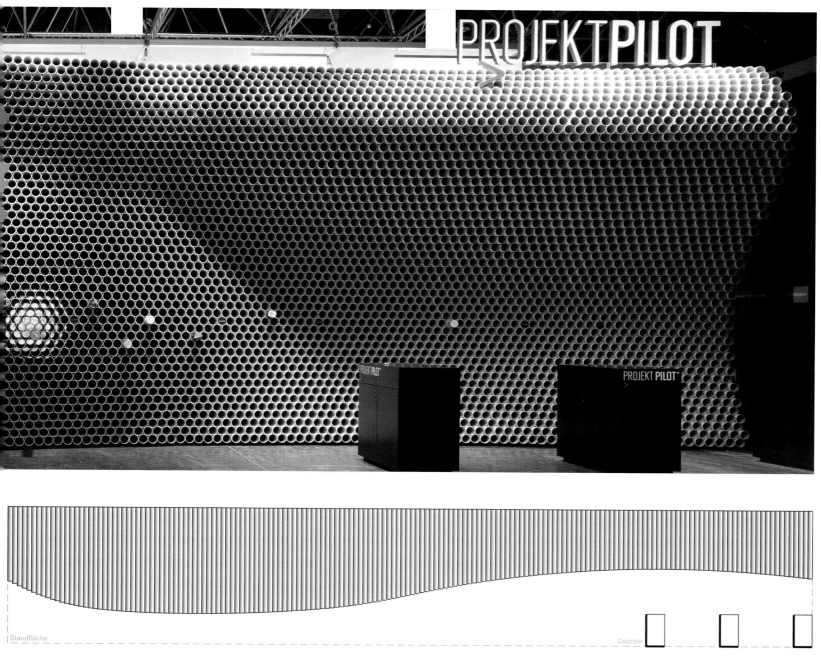

Stand plan

The stand wasn't just unusual in terms of its proportions (10 x 54 ft), but also in terms of the material used: cardboard tubes were stacked individually to form a large organic-shaped construction.

Cardboard Cloud

Oslo, Norway June 22–August 23, 2009

© Fantastic Norway

The "Cardboard Cloud" is an exhibition commissioned by the Centre for Design and Architecture (DogA) in Oslo, Norway. The exhibition displays work produced by Norwegian design students. The architectural framework for the exhibition, designed by Fantastic Norway Architects, presents new design objects. The installation was conceived around the idea of unpacking and the thrill motivated by this action.

It consisted of more than three thousand hanging cardboard boxes of different shapes and sizes assembled together to form a large "pixilated cloud," hovering over the exhibition space.

The installation served as support for the exhibited objects that were displayed inside, outside, and around the boxes. It also generated a sequence of spaces and paths organized inside the 3,767 sq ft exhibition hall.

The objects and design concepts were exhibited both inside and outside the boxes.

Show: **5X70m²**
Category: **Exhibition design**
Designer: **Fantastic Norway**
Client: **Centre for Design and Architecture (DogA)**
Area: **3,767 sq ft**
Cost: **€6,000**

From an environmental perspective, the ambition was to create an exhibition with focus on reuse and low material cost. The cardboard boxes were recycled at the end of the exhibition, which left only wires as leftovers.

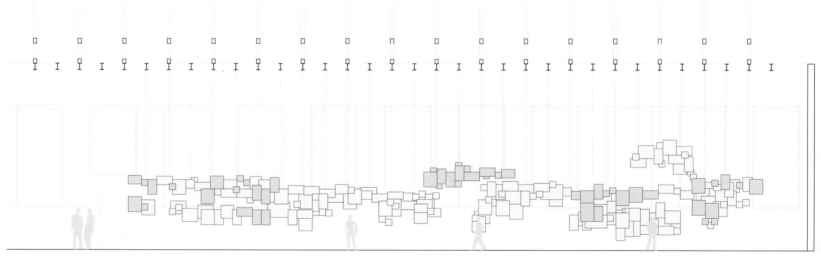

Gallery longitudinal section

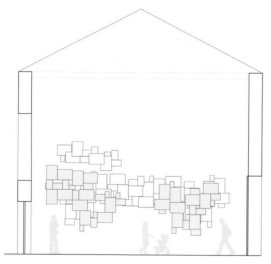

Gallery cross section

D5 Exhibition

Langenthal, Switzerland 2006

© Denz

For this design exhibition, the firm Denz was granted a 6,400 sq ft space in a warehouse. The architects divided it into three areas: exhibition, lounge, and information zone. The first was used to present a single product: the new D5 storage system. The versatility of the product was sufficient to make it the predominant element of the exhibition, and therefore, little visual support was needed other than three vending machines, stacks of the product's packaging boxes, and piles of cardboard tubes and paper rolls. The single long row of shelves blended perfectly in the gray industrial environment, and nonetheless the designer group successfully conveyed the message about the versatility of the product.

D5's program is in its name: office, library, shop, directional signage, and home living are the five main functions and application markets. Yet, D5 is also, as shown in the warehouse, an architectural element for structuring the room and a system for text and directional signs. This latter was used effectively to bring out the domestic application of the system: *la vie est dure sans confiture*, (French for "life is hard without jam.")

Show: **Designers' Saturday**
Category: **Trade show design**
Designer: **Gessaga Hindermann**
Client: **Denz**
Area: **6,400 sq ft**
Cost: **Not available**

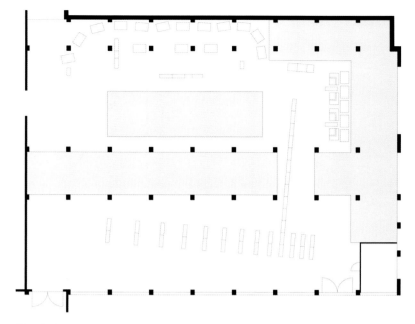

Stand plan

The Traffic of Clouds

Berlin, Germany September through October 2007

© Hans-Georg Gaul

Created in collaboration with Norwegian artist Jan Christensen, who was responsible for the paintings, this site-specific installation blurred the boundaries between adjacent spaces of PROGRAM's gallery and offices by means of interwoven wood boards. With no attachments, the tension generated by the boards was sufficient to create a stable structure that flowed through the spaces. The "Traffic of Clouds" aimed to redefine the preconceived ways people use spaces on a daily basis. As a result, the structure provided a succession of sitting areas and work surfaces. Just as the limits of the different spaces were blurred, so was the purpose of the structure, which was an installation object, walking surface, and room simultaneously. Both the built form and the wall painting expressed a sense of constant movement. Jan Christensen's painting deepened the space of the rooms—blending color into changing views. Christensen recaptured the spirit of urban wall painting and graffiti by overstepping the formal boundaries of the gallery's walls. As if in dialogue with the movement of the boards, multihued patterns spread indistinctively across walls, ceiling, and column.

Show: **Urban Nomads**
Category: **Installation**
Designer: **Hackenbroich Architekten**
Client: **PROGRAM Gallery**
Area: **1,722 sq ft**
Cost: **€9,000**

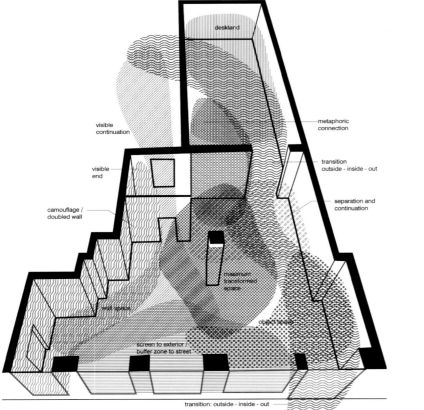

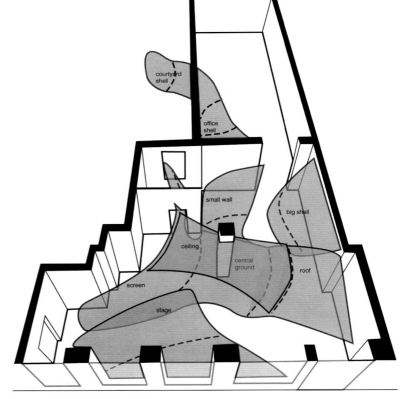

Spatial configuration based on the context and the resulting divisions

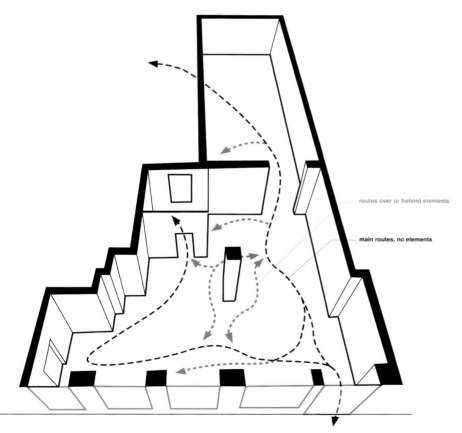

routes over or behind elements

main routes, no elements

Circulation through the installation

Those working in PROGRAM's office were invited to use the structure as an office throughout the duration of the exhibition. Wi-Fi use was also available for visitors during the exhibition hours.

1

2

3

4

5

6

7

8

9

10

11

12

Exhibition Giveaway: The TOC Do-It-Yourself Kit

Paper Bag Igloo

Chuo-ku, Tokyo, Japan   October 14–25, 2008

© Yasutaka Yoshimura Architects

Yasutaka Yoshimura Architects designed this exhibition at an art bookstore in Tokyo around the concept of a book they had published two years earlier: *Super Legal Buildings*. Before focusing on the design of the exhibit, it is worth mentioning that the book mainly deals with Tokyo's building codes and responds to the question, why are Tokyo's buildings so abstract? The book was printed in two colors and the architects received many requests from readers about wanting to see the photos in full-color. The exhibit was to respond to this request, and the architects' original idea consisted of showing the pictures as big as possible by means of a projector. But there was one problem: The gallery was in a space adjacent to the bookstore, and a solution needed to be found to make this space dark. A screen was then created that served to block the light while also receiving the projected image. The material for the screen was a generic white paper bag used at the bookstore. By unfolding and stacking rows of paper bags, the goal was achieved, and it took the shape of an igloo-like shelter.

Show: **Display of photographs from the book *Super Legal Buildings***
Category: **Temporary installation**
Designer: **Yasutaka Yoshimura Architects**
Client: **Morioka Shoten**
Area: **139 sq ft**
Cost: **Approx. €260**

TECHTILE

Tokyo, Japan November 23–27, 2007

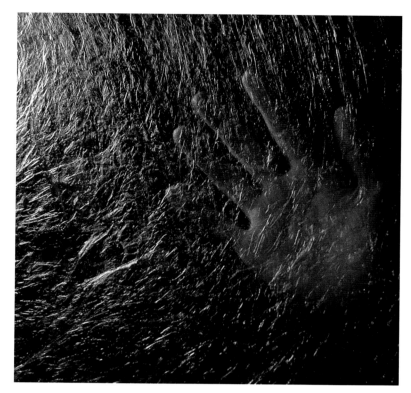

© NOSIGNER

"For me, the most important things in design are invisible—the way a person feels when using a product or the intentions under which the design is produced" (from an interview by Terri Peters for *Metropolis* magazine). With these words the artist and designer NOSIGNER describes his work. Environmental issues are often a topic present in his creations. In collaboration with Yasuaki Kakehi and Masashi Nakatani, NOSIGNER created a space about the tactile sensation of ice. The large ice-like installation was made out of 32,810 ft of plastic wrap. When sixteen layers of the films are compressed, it looks like thin ice with cracks. Lighting and sound effects were used to convey the feeling of cold. In spite of the low cost of the materials used, the result was ingenious and artful. Actually, everyone was surprised that the room felt like the inside of an ice chamber. Because of the unique way of making the space and also the extremely low cost of the design, it was awarded the Design for Asia Silver Award, which is the highest prize for exhibition design.

Show: **TECHTILE**
Category: **Exhibition design**
Designer: **NOSIGNER**
Client: **TECHTILE Exhibition Executive Committee**
Area: **581.25 sq ft**
Cost: **$22 per sq ft**

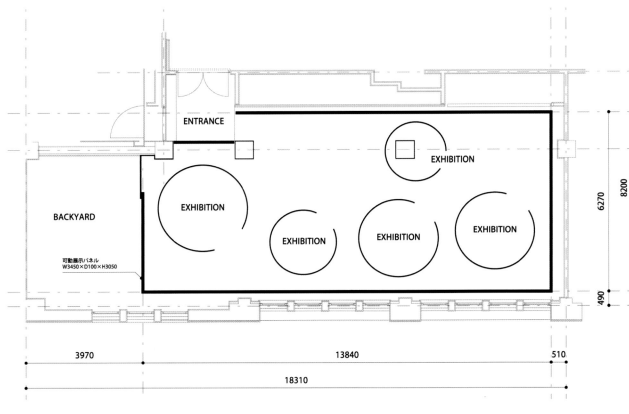

Stand plan

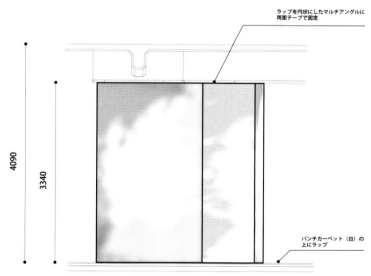

ラップを円状にしたマルチアングルに
両面テープで固定

パンチカーペット（白）の
上にラップ

4090

3340

Partial elevation

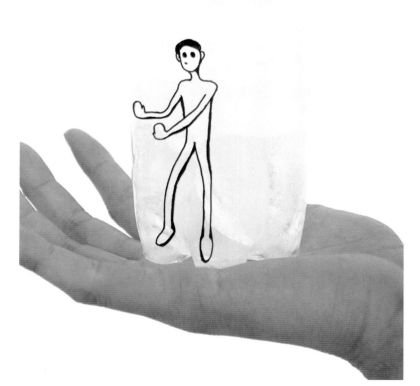

MAD in China

Copenhagen, Denmark
November 3, 2007–January 6, 2008

© Danish Architecture Center

"Mad in China" was a solo design exhibition of the Beijing-based architecture office MAD, at the Danish Architecture Center (DAC) in Copenhagen. That was the second exhibition of MAD in Europe, after attending the Venice Architecture Biennial in 2006. Kent Martinussen, director of DAC, remarked that "Mad in China is not merely an exhibition of an emerging new firm. Rather, the firm's controversial social dimension brings new perspective on China to the West. China begins to make their own rules, no longer subject to the taste of foreign countries."

The show featured projects like the visionary "Beijing 2050," a futuristic foresight for a densely populated city in the year 2050, that includes transforming Tiananmen Square into a green parkland.

The display of models and information panels about various projects—built or unbuilt—were like the architecture the firm is known for creating: astonishing and daring in the context of the museum's old wooden structure. Sleek bases suspended from the ceiling by metallic struts were used to support the meticulously fabricated scale models, while a large digital image covered the entry wall to the exhibition, representing the threshold to a futuristic vision of the world.

Show: **Danish Architecture Center**
Category: **Exhibition design**
Designer: **Danish Architecture Center**
Client: **Danish Architecture Center**
Area: **Not available**
Cost: **Not available**

Contrast was created by the juxtaposition of futuristic imagery and modern materials with the gallery space, characterized by the museum's massive wood columns and ceiling trusses.

Mutagenesis

Verona, Italy September 20–24, 2007

© Saverio Lombardi Vallauri, Milano

Mutagenesis is the term used in genetics for the production of mutations in DNA. It is also the theme that inspired the designer to create a space filled with brightly painted wood plank sculptures that interacted like mutagens. "Mutagenesis," a solo exhibition by Arne Quinze, was structured around the concepts "Artifacts of today" and "Artifacts of the future." The exhibition explored concepts of movement captured in time and space.

On the occasion of this exhibition, Quinze's wooden sculptures served as background to his own fantastic projects. The pieces included Stilt Houses (raised structures of painted timber planks), Bond (a range of organic sculptural pieces), Magna (a futuristic vehicle powered by a magnetic jet engine), and Skytracer (some kind of boomerang thing).

Show: **Abitare il Tempo**
Category: **Exhibition design**
Designer: **Arne Quinze**
Client: **Arne Quinze**
Area: **43,060 sq ft**
Cost: **Not available**

The planks of his wood constructions never constitute contained forms, which are nailed together randomly, as if they were three-dimensional sketches.

"Artifacts of today" expressed Quinze's vision for a way of life translated into realized design objects; "Artifacts of the future" presented a range of futuristic sculptures like never-ending mutations found in nature.

Oxygen Bubbles

Linz, Austria 2006

© Dietmar Tollerian

The designers' conceptual goal for this exhibition of their own work was to add value to ordinary elements by taking them out of their usual context and imbuing them with the quality of an artistic creation. Two items were chosen to achieve this goal: Fiber cement panels, a strong material often used in construction, and clear inflatable PVC cubes of different sizes (47 x 59 x 43 in).

Vertical "Eternity" panels were hanging from the ceiling only a few inches above the floor. They swung slightly with the breeze like tree leaves.

Architectural models were displayed inside PVC bubbles placed throughout the gallery space. These bubbles replaced the common Plexiglas showcases and appeared, in their softness, contradictory to the displayed models. The combination of presentation techniques was calculated to cause "amazement" in the viewers as soon as they entered the room. The presentation was reinforced by the neutral background of the gallery space: gray flooring, white walls, and backlit ceiling that illuminated the space uniformly.

Show: **Lentos Art Museum**
Category: **Exhibition design**
Designer: **Caramel Architekten**
Client: **Lentos Art Museum**
Area: **9,900 sq ft**
Cost: **€25,000**

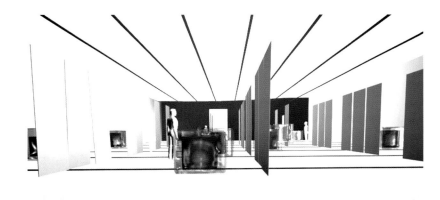

Computer-generated rendering

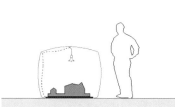

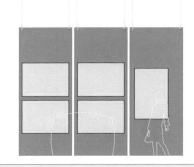

Partial elevation

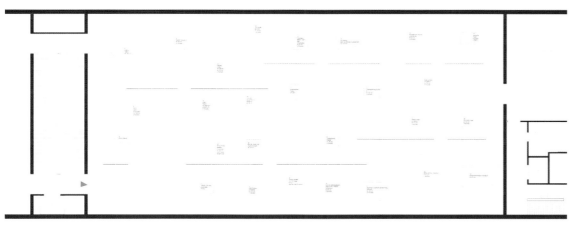

Exhibition plan

Made in Italy files

Rome, Italy May 8–27, 2007

© Danish Architecture Center

This exhibition was located in Rome's fascinating Domitian's Stadium. Made of travertine stone, it is the only example of a stone stadium from the Roman Empire. It was 902 ft long and 348 ft wide. Later, it became the footprint of Piazza Navona, which follows the shape of Domitian's stadium underneath it.

The organizers' intention was to establish a contrast between the brightly colored contemporary materials and the archaeological stone treasures which surrounded them. A large red wall and an elevated footbridge organized the space and led visitors through the exhibition. The simplicity of the design emphasized the contrast between the massive Roman structure as the container and the footbridge inserted in it.

The route was punctuated by pedestals for the display of architectural scale models. The footbridge represented a relatively large investment, but this was compensated for by its potential long-term use for future exhibitions with similar characteristics.

Show: **Domitian's Stadium**
Category: **Exhibition design**
Designer: **Danish Architecture Center**
Client: **Not available**
Area: **Not available**
Cost: **Not available**

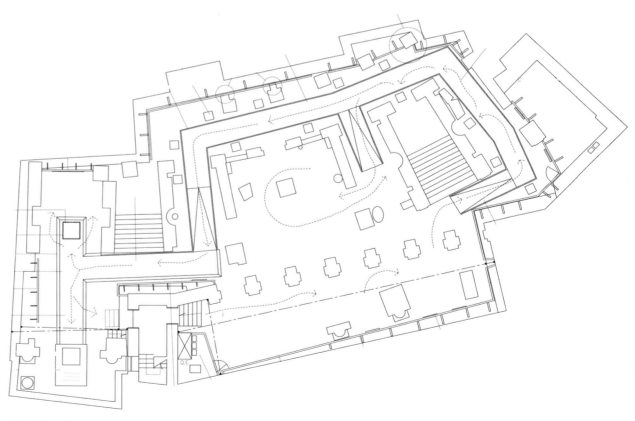

Exhibition plan

[Wide] Band

Los Angeles, CA, USA 2006

© Griffin Enright Architects

Among the selection of projects included in this book, "[Wide] Band" is certainly one of the most expensive. However, it is worth mentioning that this installation has a function beyond that of a display case or an art piece. Originally designed as an installation commissioned by NeoCon West and *Interior Design* magazine, it has been moved to the A+D Museum in Los Angeles where it functions as a café. It is a space where users can consult their e-mails, get together, or just enjoy a break from their professional activity. With an orange surface that folds over on itself, the space is surrounded by the panel that lends the project its name.

The name is inspired by both the physical presence of the installation and by the broadband technology that supports the wireless Internet access provided. "[Wide]Band" is an exploration of a continuous surface that loops around to create floors, walls, and ceilings. Users are drawn to the long table that punctuates the interior space of the loop. The space that contains the installation is emblazoned with "[Wide]Band" in 9-ft-tall letters, whose effect shifts from legible to abstractly graphic as one moves through the installation.

Show: **NeoCon West**
Category: **Installation**
Designer: **Griffin Enright Architects**
Client: *Interior Design* **magazine, NeoCon West and A+D Museum in Los Angeles**
Area: **600 sq ft**
Cost: **$15,000 worth of donated materials. All labor was donated.**

The primary material was orange ¾ in polycarbonate core paneling chosen for its structural capacity to span large spaces and for its translucency. The panels are supported only by a steel skeleton of 1 ½ in; in some places extending beyond the frame.

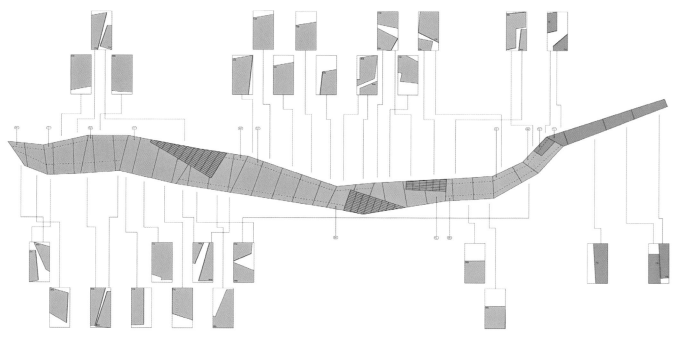

Unfolded stand plan

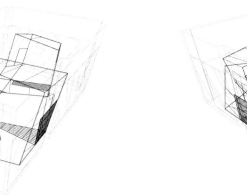

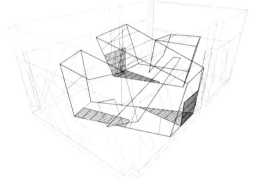

Computer-generated three-dimensional views

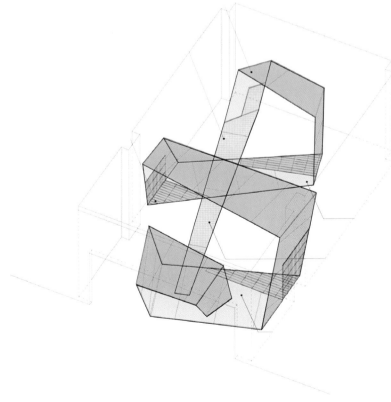

Color-rendered stand inserted in the exhibition space

Canopy

Long Island City, NY, USA 2004

© nARCHITECTS

"Canopy" was a temporary structure built in the courtyard of the P.S.1 Contemporary Art Center on the occasion of the summer activities program to accommodate day and evening events.

The architects wanted to experiment with bamboo as a construction material and used it to create a metaphor for the foliage of a densely forested area. Before the construction, the group of architects and architecture students who participated in the project studied the physical properties of the material, especially the degree of humidity that would allow for optimal manipulation. The architects explored the design possibilities to provide overhead shade, seating, and varying atmospheres. Covering a large part of the center's courtyard, a lattice of bamboo arcs generated a sequence of vaulted spaces and areas open to the sky while producing a range of shadow densities and patterns across the ground. As a result, four different zones were created: "Pool Pad," the largest of the spaces, included a shallow pool; "Fog Pad" was an area where fog nozzles spread a cool halo of mist; "Rainforest" was a sound environment, with water misters that re-created a living bamboo forest; finally, "Sand Hump" was a beach oriented to maximize exposure to sun and shade.

Show: **P.S.1 Contemporary Art Center**
Category: **Installation**
Designer: **nARCHITECTS**
Client: **MoMA/P.S.1 Young Architects Program**
Area: **Not available**
Cost: **Not available**

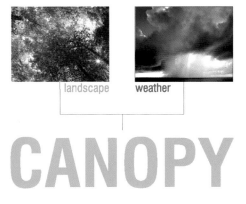

landscape   weather

CANOPY

A canopy built with freshly cut green bamboo turns from green to tan over the summer

Dips in the canopy provoke different modes of lounging in four distinct environments.

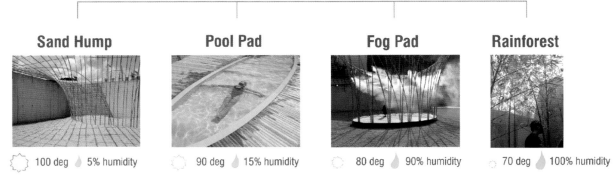

Sand Hump   **Pool Pad**   **Fog Pad**   **Rainforest**

100 deg   5% humidity   90 deg   15% humidity   80 deg   90% humidity   70 deg   100% humidity

Pinches in the canopy produce a range of shadow densities.

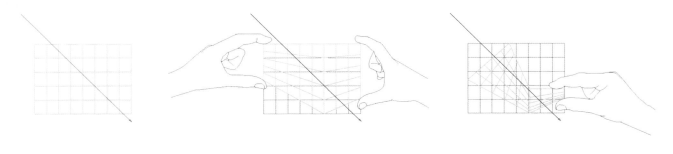

July 21st: 11:00...   *... 2:00*   *... 6:00*

Conceptual diagrams

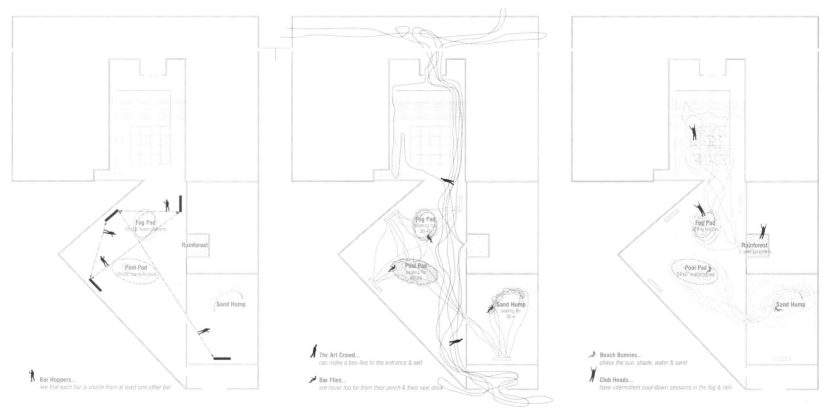

Bar Hoppers...
like that each bar is visible from at least one other bar

The Art Crowd...
can make a bee-line to the entrance & exit

Bar Flies...
are never too far from their perch & their next drink

Beach Bunnies...
chase the sun, shade, water & sand

Club Heads...
have intermittent cool-down sessions in the fog & rain

User diagrams

These spaces are the backdrops to the various recreational activities planned during a hot summer in the city. Families with children were attracted to the day activities, while numerous parties were organized for the evenings.

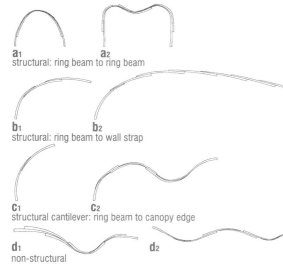

a₁   **a₂**
structural: ring beam to ring beam

b₁   **b₂**
structural: ring beam to wall strap

c₁   **c₂**
structural cantilever: ring beam to canopy edge

d₁   **d₂**
non-structural

Splice types

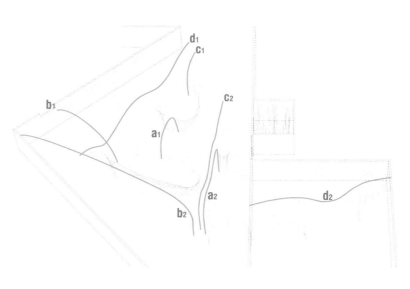

Mirror Error

Meiji-jingu Shinjuku-ku, Tokyo, Japan
November 2–6, 2005

© Daici Ano

The mail-order furniture magazine *House Styling* commissioned Yasutaka Yoshimura Architects to design a booth for the 2005 edition of Tokyo Design Week. The magazine decided that the stand should be in the area called "container exhibition," a site filled with cargo containers that the event organizers make available for use as exhibition stands. In this case, the architects chose the most deteriorated—and therefore the cheapest—container available. Because this container was to be removed from the site after the exhibition, it was possible to drill a constellation of holes of different sizes throughout its walls. This offered an excellent opportunity for an interactive setup that involved the contents of the steel box and the visitor. The interior of the container, which was not accessible to visitors, held various pieces of furniture. A game was proposed to the visitors: peeping through the holes, visitors had to match the items displayed in the interior of the container with the corresponding images shown in the catalog.

Show: **Tokio Design Week**
Category: **Temporary installation**
Designer: **Yasutaka Yoshimura Architects**
Client: *House Styling*
Area: **320 sq ft**
Cost: **Approx. €3,600**

The trick: Similar pieces of the same line were paired up (see legend). The viewer had to "spot the difference" before identifying the items in the company's catalog. The catch: the architects succeeded in drawing the visitors' attention to the magazine.

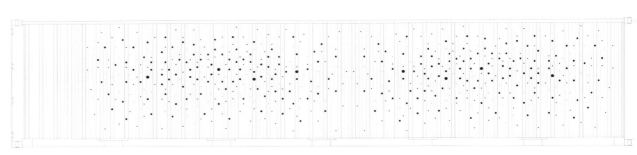

Container long elevation

Container plan

1 . Skiima sofa 1 Sheeter black
1*. Skiima sofa 1 Sheeter brown
2 . Snow table square
2*. Snow table rectangular
3 . Disk
4 . Mop chest 25 drawer
5 . Slit rack chest
6 . PePe side chair
7 . Butterfly stool

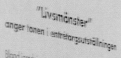

"Livsmönster"
anger tonen i entretorgsutställningen

Bland inredningstrenderna som har kommit under
de senaste säsongerna är en trend särskilt påfal-
lande och allmängiltig; mönster.
Entretorgsutställningen har gestaltats av arkitekt-
gruppen Marge i samarbete med Paula Malm AB.
Marge jobbar med bostäder, utredningar och
inredning och har bland annat gjort sig ett namn
genom inredningen av Moderna Museet 2004.

Marge har byggt upp ett metaforiskt landskap av
stora sittelement som bildar olika nivåer. Ovanför
landskapet svävar en stor tyg ram, som, om man
står på en av landskapets högsta punkter, bildar en
rumslighet.

I utställningen finns även en liten lägenhet i vilken
det bor en fiktiv person, en man med en alldeles
egen, personlig stil. Vi vill presentera er genom
boendemiljö i stället får en färgkoordinerad trend-
ställning, säger Paula Malm, trendkonsult.

Formex

Estocolmo, Suecia 2003

© Johan Fowelin, Magnus Skoglöf

During its fourteen years of history, Formex, a gift and handicrafts trade show has built up a reputation as one of the most important events in Sweden. Given his showcase character for new trends that attracts a large audience, the event confers a special importance to signage and communication.

Marge was commissioned to create a stand that would serve as a visual reference and could accommodate a large number of visitors. To avoid long lines at the front desk, the architects chose to create a 4,300 sq ft booth with a simple circulation plan that included the main access on a side and the exit facing the other stands. To avoid big crowds in specific areas, this route branched out to other parts of the stand such as the lounge, the information desks, an exhibition space, and various intermediate spaces with panels and other objects.

Above the central area of the stand hovered a gigantic square white lampshade. Interestingly enough, this element had no logo or word printed on it, as one would expect. Instead, this unexpected brightness in the midst of the tumultuous atmosphere of the fair catched the eye of visitors from a distance. This strategy allowed the stand to become a landmark in the exhibition premises and unified the various elements of the stand.

Show: **Formex**
Category: **Trade show design**
Designer: **Marge Architecten**
Client: **Not available**
Area: **Approx. 4,300 sq ft**
Cost: **Not available**

The floating white frame tied all the different zones of the stand together and echoed the colorful square display area that acted as the heart of the stand, where most activity took place.

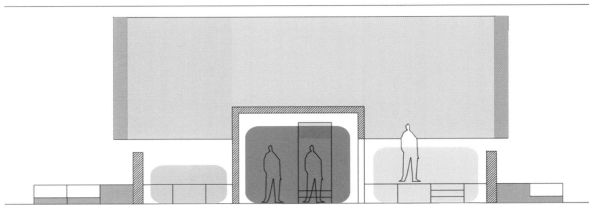

Stand schematic elevation

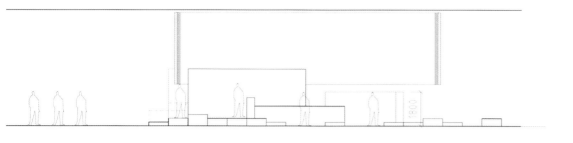

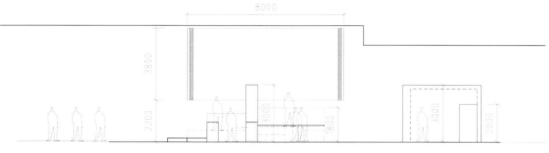

Sections

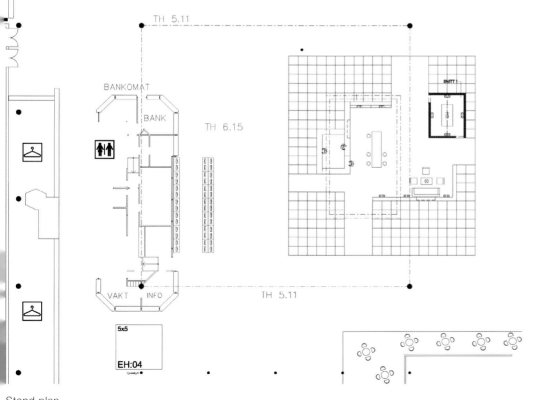

Stand plan

Directory

Andrew Maynard Architects
Melbourne, Australia
www.andrewmaynard.com.au

BAAS
Barcelona, Spain
www.jordibadia.com

Bosch & Fjord
Copenhagen, Denmark
www.bosch-fjord.com

Caramel Architekten
Vienna, Austria
www.caramel.at

D'ART DESIGN GRUPPE
Neuss, Germany
www.dartdesign.de

Danish Architecture Center
Copenhagen, Denmark
http://english.dac.dk

Gessaga Hindermann
Zürich, Switzerland
www.designrichtung.ch

Dylan Kwok
Helsinki, Finland
www.dylankwok.com

Estudi Arola
Barcelona, Spain
www.estudiarola.com

Fantastic Norway
Oslo, Norway
www.fantasticnorway.no

Griffin Enright Architects
Los Angeles, CA, USA
www.griffinenrightarchitects.com

HAAG WAGNER
Zürich, Switzerland
www.haagwagner.ch

Hackenbroich Architekten
Berlin, Germany
www.hackenbroich.com

J. MAYER H.
Berlin, Germany
www.jmayerh.de

Marge Architecten
Rotterdam, the Netherlands
www.marge-architecten.nl

Maurice Mentjens Design
Holtum, the Netherlands
www.mauricementjens.com

nARCHITECTS
Brooklyn, NY, USA
www.narchitects.com

NOSIGNER
Tokyo, Japan
www.nosigner.com

Quinze & Milan
Kortrijk, Belgium
www.quinzeandmilan.tv

Ronan & Erwan Bouroullec
Paris, France
www.bouroullec.com

Sagan Piechota Architecture
San Francisco, CA, USA
www.sp-architecture.com

UpO Architettura/Viabizzuno
Bologna, Italy
www.viabizzuno.com

vc a
Milan, Italy
http://www.vc-a.it

XRANGE
Taipei, Taiwan
www.xrange.net

Yasutaka Yoshimura Architects
Tokyo, Japan
www.ysmr.com